BLAZERS

CRIME SOLVERS

FINDING THE

MURDER WEAPON

by Melissa Langley Biegert

Consultant:
David Foran, PhD
Director, Forensic Science Program
Michigan State University

Reading Consultant:
Barbara J. Fox
Reading Specialist
North Carolina State University

Capstone
press

Mankato, Minnesota

Blazers is published by Capstone Press,
151 Good Counsel Drive, P.O. Box 669, Mankato, Minnesota 56002.
www.capstonepress.com

Books published by Capstone Press are manufactured with paper
containing at least 10 percent post-consumer waste.

Library of Congress Cataloging-in-Publication Data
Biegert, Melissa Ann Langley, 1967–
    Finding the murder weapon / by Melissa Langley Biegert.
    p. cm. — (Blazers. Crime solvers)
    Includes bibliographical references and index.
    Summary: "Describes methods used by experts to find murder weapons to solve crimes" —
Provided by publisher.
    ISBN 978-1-4296-3374-1 (library binding)
    1. Murder — Investigation — Juvenile literature. 2. Evidence, Criminal — Juvenile
literature. 3. Criminal investigation — Vocational guidance — Juvenile literature. I. Title.
II. Series.
HV8079.H6B52 2010
363.25'2 — dc22   2009014605

Editorial Credits
Megan Schoeneberger, editor; Matt Bruning, designer; Eric Gohl, media researcher

Photo Credits
AP Images/Bill Greene, Pool, 29; Steve Pope, 24–25; Toby Talbot, 18
Capstone Press/Karon Dubke, badge (all), cover (all), 4, 5, 13, 14–15
Getty Images Inc./Aurora/Ron Koeberer, 12; Michael Williams, 21; Riser/Zigy Kaluzny, 27
iStockphoto/tillsonburg, 6
Photo Researchers, Inc/Edward Kinsman, 23
Shutterstock/AVAVA, 16; Dale A Stork, 9; Derek Thomas, 22 (top); Dino O., 22 (bottom);
    ene, 26; Jack Dagley Photography, 11; Kirsty Pargeter, 19; Leah-Anne Thompson, 17;
    Loren Rodgers, 10; Mushakesa, bullet holes (all), 8 (all); PeJo, 7; Péter Gudella, 30

CRIME SOLVERS

FINDING THE MURDER WEAPON

TABLE OF CONTENTS

no. 213900192

CHAPTER ONE

WHO DID IT?

Someone has been murdered! A body lies in a pool of blood. But the killer is nowhere to be found.

CROSS   POLICE LINE DO NOT CROSS

Detectives arrive at the scene. They search for **evidence** to track down the killer. To solve the crime, they'll need to find the murder **weapon**.

evidence – information, items, and facts that help prove something to be true or false

weapon – something used to injure or harm

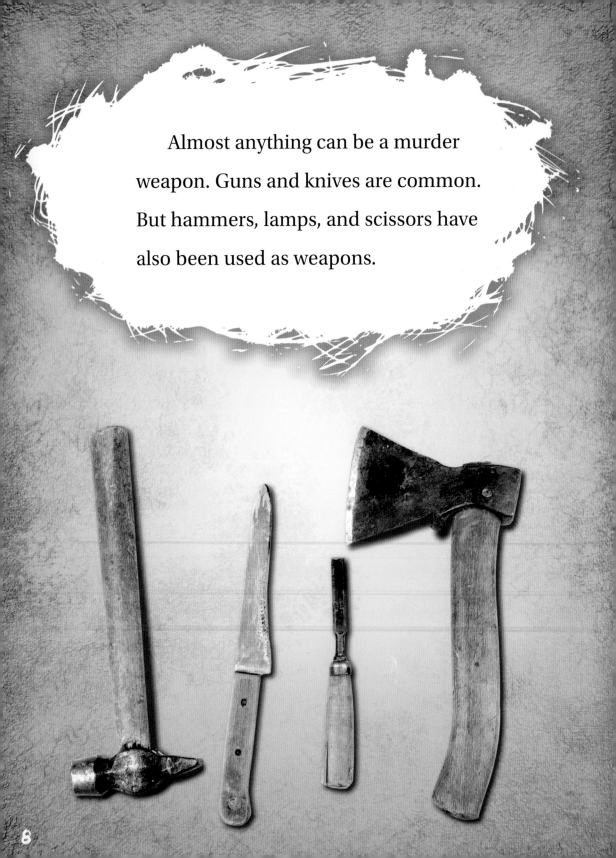

Almost anything can be a murder weapon. Guns and knives are common. But hammers, lamps, and scissors have also been used as weapons.

BLAZERS FACT

More than two-thirds of all murders in the United States involve guns.

CHAPTER TWO

ON THE SCENE

Detectives look closely at the **victim** for clues. Was the victim stabbed, shot, or choked? Clues tell detectives what kind of weapon might have been used.

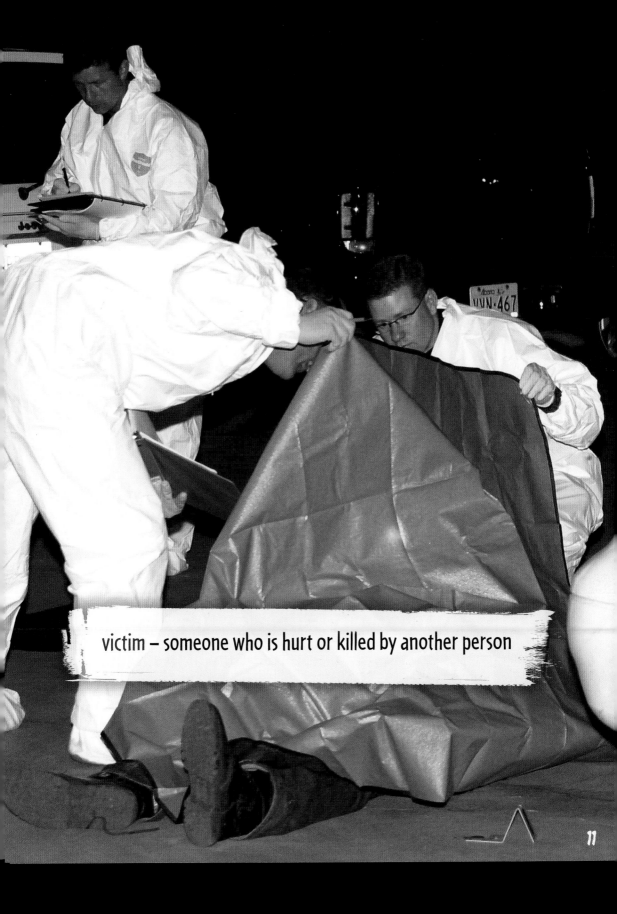

victim – someone who is hurt or killed by another person

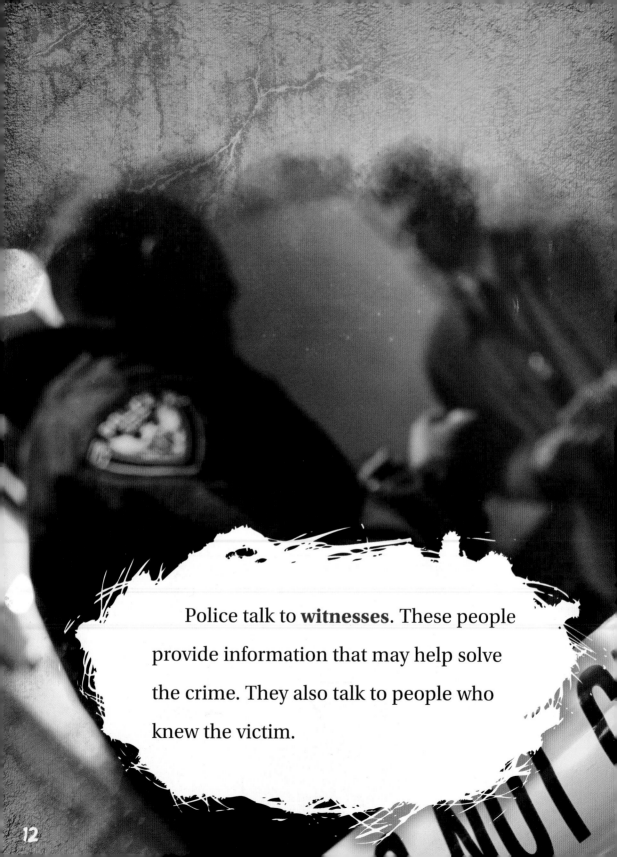

Police talk to **witnesses**. These people provide information that may help solve the crime. They also talk to people who knew the victim.

witness – someone who observes events related to a crime

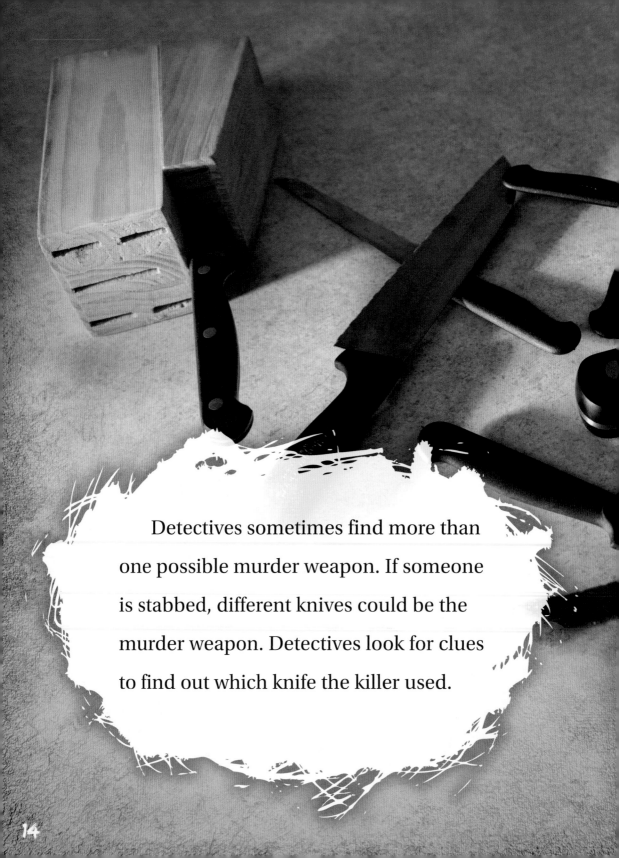

Detectives sometimes find more than one possible murder weapon. If someone is stabbed, different knives could be the murder weapon. Detectives look for clues to find out which knife the killer used.

BLAZERS FACT

In 1893, Lizzie Borden was found not guilty of killing her parents. The jury did not believe police had the correct murder weapon.

CHAPTER THREE

IN THE LAB

Detectives bring possible murder weapons to a crime lab. Lab workers test each weapon for dried blood. They need to find out whose blood it is.

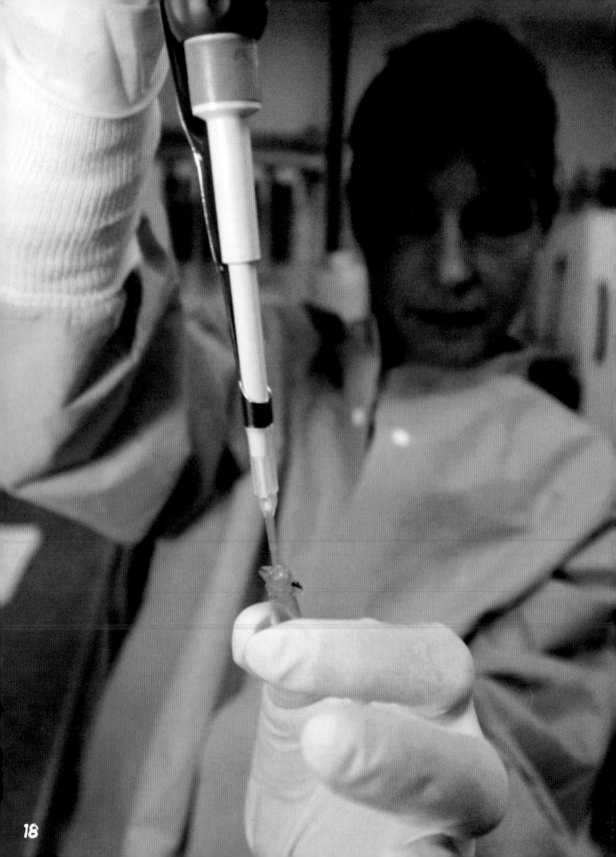

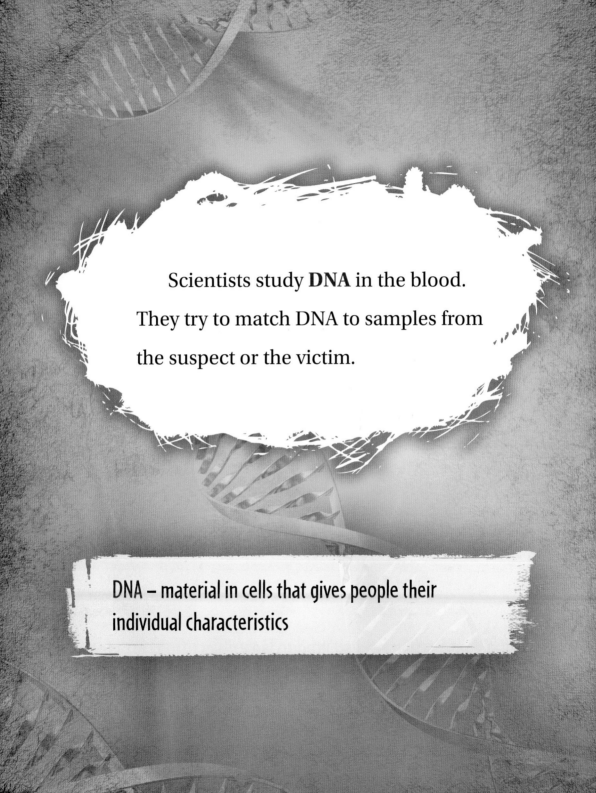

Scientists study **DNA** in the blood. They try to match DNA to samples from the suspect or the victim.

DNA – material in cells that gives people their individual characteristics

Lab workers use **microscopes** to compare weapons to wounds. Weapons often have tiny marks on them. Workers compare the marks to the wounds. This information can help determine if a weapon was used in a crime.

microscope – a tool used to view objects too small for humans to see

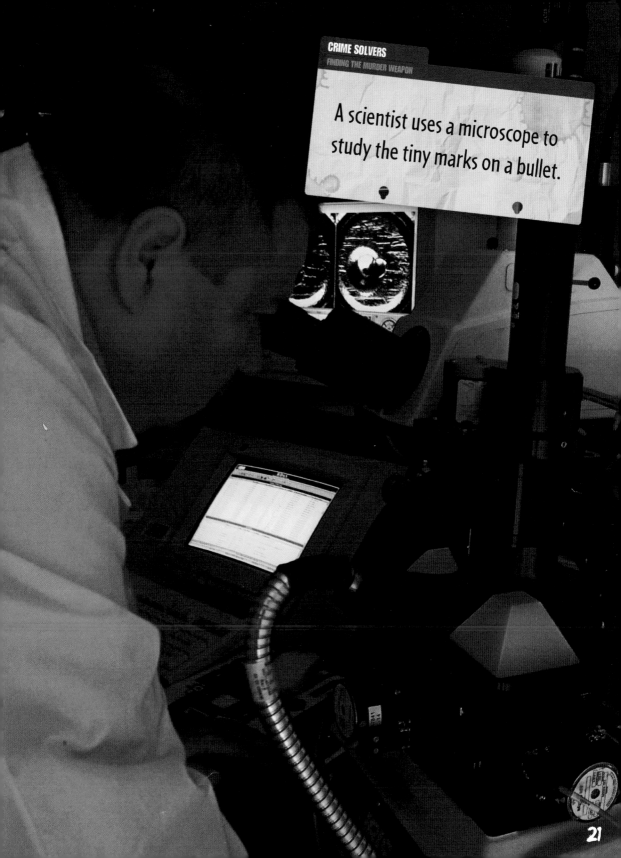

A scientist uses a microscope to study the tiny marks on a bullet.

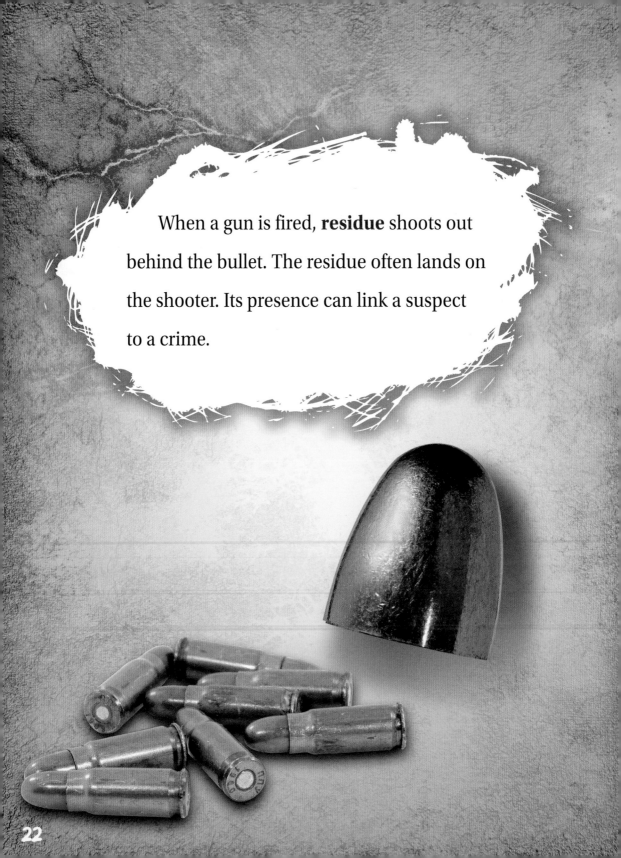

When a gun is fired, **residue** shoots out behind the bullet. The residue often lands on the shooter. Its presence can link a suspect to a crime.

residue – what is left after something burns up or evaporates

BLAZERS FACT

Every gun is different on the inside. When fired, a gun leaves marks on a bullet. Experts can match bullets to the guns that fired them.

BLAZERS FACT

Some officials want to create a national database of all guns. These computer files could help solve crimes.

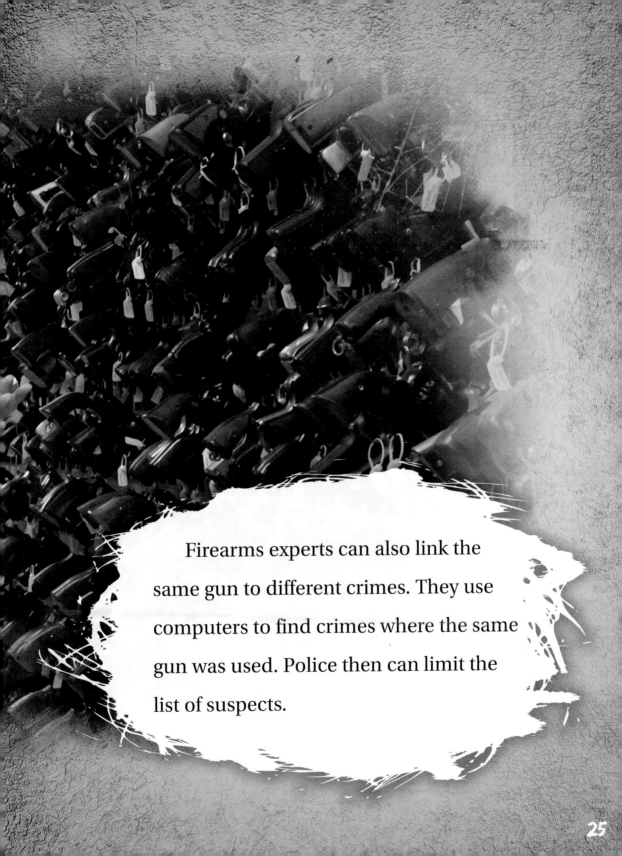

Firearms experts can also link the same gun to different crimes. They use computers to find crimes where the same gun was used. Police then can limit the list of suspects.

CHAPTER FOUR

WEAPONS, SUSPECTS, AND CRIMES

Scientists are always finding new ways to match weapons to crimes and criminals. Linking a suspect to a weapon and crime helps officials uncover the truth.

BLAZERS FACT

In 1997, Timothy McVeigh was found guilty of bombing a building in Oklahoma City. Police found materials from the bomb on McVeigh's clothing.

Officers present the murder weapon in court. The weapon is often the strongest evidence against a suspect. This evidence helps make sure killers are punished.

BLAZERS FACT

In 2007, California police solved a six-year-old murder case. They finally found the weapon buried behind the suspect's former home.

Glossary

DNA (dee-en-AYE) — material in cells that gives people their individual characteristics; DNA stands for deoxyribonucleic acid.

evidence (EV-uh-duhnss) — information, items, and facts that help prove something to be true or false

microscope (MYE-kruh-skope) — a tool that makes very small things look large enough to be seen

residue (REZ-uh-doo) — what is left after something burns up or evaporates

victim (VIK-tuhm) — someone who is hurt or killed by another person

weapon (WEP-uhn) — something used to injure or harm

witness (WIT-niss) — someone who observes events related to a crime

Read More

Herbst, Judith. *The History of Weapons.* Major Inventions through History. Minneapolis: Twenty-First Century Books, 2006.

Joyce, Jaime. *Bullet Proof!: The Evidence that Guns Leave Behind.* 24/7, Science behind the Scenes. New York: Franklin Watts, 2007.

Miller, Connie Colwell. *Crime Scene Investigators: Uncovering the Truth.* Line of Duty. Mankato, Minn.: Capstone Press, 2008.

Internet Sites

FactHound offers a safe, fun way to find Internet sites related to this book. All of the sites on FactHound have been researched by our staff.

Here's all you do:

Visit *www.facthound.com*

FactHound will fetch the best sites for you!

Index